The Baptists

by
John Wood

FOREWORD BY
REVD RAYMOND BROWN, M.A., B.D., M.TH., PH.D.
PRINCIPAL, SPURGEON'S COLLEGE

THE RELIGIOUS EDUCATION PRESS
A Division of Pergamon Press

A. Wheaton & Company Limited
A Division of Pergamon Press
Hennock Road, Exeter EX2 8RP

Pergamon Press Ltd
Headington Hill Hall, Oxford OX3 0BW

Pergamon Press Inc.
Maxwell House, Fairview Park, Elmsford, New York 10523

Pergamon of Canada Ltd
75 The East Mall, Toronto, Ontario M8Z 2L9

Pergamon Press (Australia) Pty Ltd
19a Boundary Street, Rushcutters Bay, N.S.W. 2011

Pergamon Press GmbH
6242 Kronberg/Taunus, Pferdstrasse 1,
Frankfurt-am-Main, West Germany

First edition 1977
Reprinted 1978

Printed in Great Britain by A. Wheaton & Co. Ltd, Exeter
ISBN 0 08 020911 4 flexi net
ISBN 0 08 020910 6 flexi non net

Contents

ACKNOWLEDGEMENTS

Thanks are due to the following for permission to reproduce photographs: Swedish Lutheran Mission (pages 14, 19), Baptist Union (pages 23, 24), Baptist Times (page 33), Dr R. Goulding, Association Secretary, Baptist World Alliance, London (page 39), Revd Stanley Turl (page 51), and Baptist Missionary Society (page 52).

COVER PHOTOGRAPH: *Baptism at Jacutinga, Brazil. By kind permission of the Baptist Missionary Society.*

Foreword

Baptists are no more responsible for their denominational label than the Quakers and the Methodists, but they are not ashamed of it. I have enjoyed reading John Wood's introduction to the life and thought of the Baptist people and I am sure that its careful study will help people of other denominations, and also those readers who at present have no clear faith, to understand the things we treasure. Obviously our greatest pride is that we belong to the company of all God's people, but it is good to know what other Christians hold dear and I am sure that this series of books will be of immense value. No denomination has a monopoly either of the truth or of the saints. There is so much for us still to learn from one another. These books will surely do much to deepen our understanding of other believers.

Raymond Brown
Principal, Spurgeon's College

1

Allow Me
to
Introduce You

It started as a nickname – much as the name 'Christian' itself began. Villagers would join a group of people standing by a river or pond to watch grown men and women being plunged beneath the water in a religious ceremony, and they would call such people 'Baptists'. As happens with so many nicknames, the label stuck!

But there is a great deal more to the Baptists than this. From the very beginning they have been champions of religious freedom. And for the past two hundred years they have helped to pioneer the missionary movement which has influenced practically every developing country in the world.

During the past four centuries the Baptists have been one of the most thorough-going reforming denominations of the Christian Church. Like some other groups they began by trying to re-form the Church as much as possible to make it like the Church in New Testament times. For Baptists this meant abandoning some time-honoured customs and practices; the Church was to be composed only of believing Christians, there was to be no more baptising of babies, and no one but Jesus Christ was to govern the religious life of each local congregation.

This book tells how their main ideas developed stage by stage, and tries to show how they differ from some other Christian denominations. The idea behind this is not to be argumentative, but to make the issues as clear as possible so that the reader can make up his or her mind about them. It is one of the healthy features of modern Church life that members of all denominations can discuss their differences openly without trying to claim that their particular Church alone is right while others are completely wrong.

We have called this book 'The Baptists' rather than 'The Baptist Church'. But this does not imply that Baptist people are such individualists that they have no concern for each other or for the wider Church as a whole. On the contrary: Baptists believe very strongly in the importance of the local churches as the means by which Christ makes his presence felt in the modern world.

Their churches come in all shapes and sizes. Most are fairly small companies of people, but some are quite large. The Moscow Baptist Church has about 5000 members. The First Baptist Church in Dallas, Texas, has a membership of 18 000. With a total of some thirty-three million members throughout the world, Baptists can claim that they are one of the largest of all Christian bodies.

The following map and table will give some idea of the distribution of Baptist members throughout the world. But certain points need to be borne in mind:

1. The figures do not include several million independent Baptists in many countries – including Russia.

2. Nor do they include the number of children and young people who attend Baptist Churches but have not yet become full members.

3. Nor can they possibly include the memberships of other Churches which hold Baptist beliefs but do not call themselves Baptists.

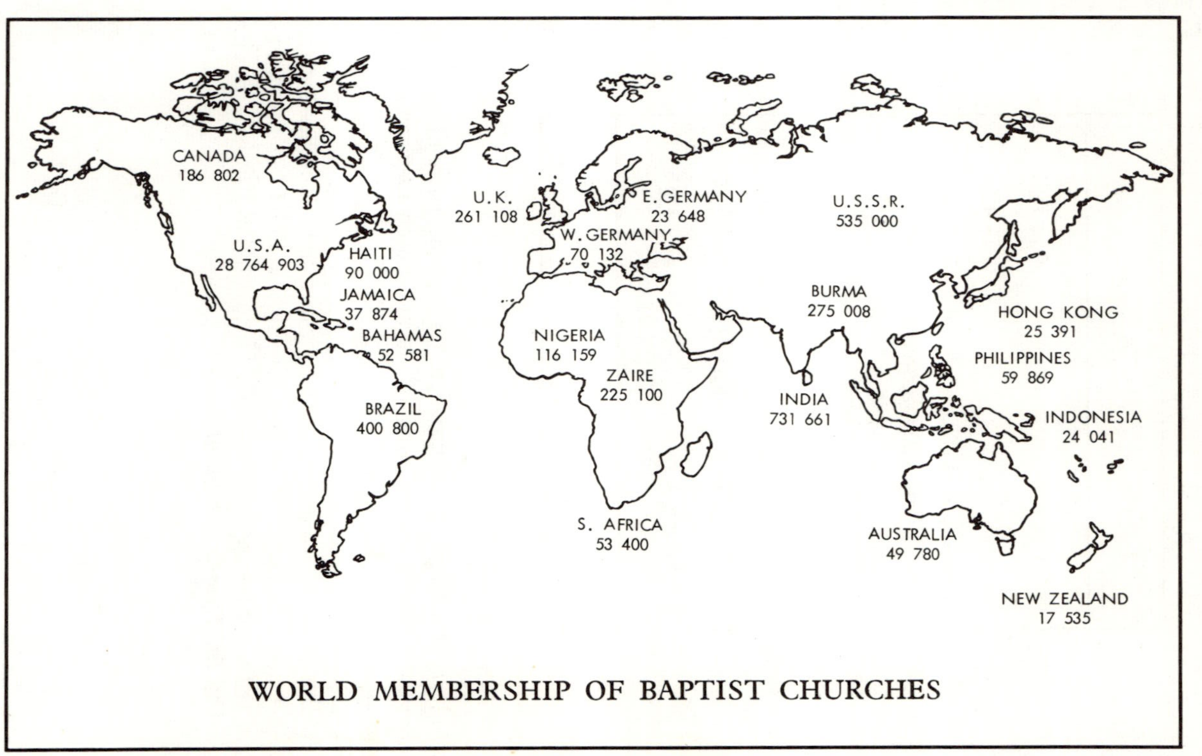

WORLD MEMBERSHIP OF BAPTIST CHURCHES

Area	Total
Africa	652 198
Asia	1 134 476
Central America and Caribbean	234 579
Europe	1 141 214
Middle East	1 369
North America	29 013 168
Oceania (Far East)	165 225
South America	462 169
Grand Total	32 804 398

Figures published by the Baptist World Alliance 1974

It is important to realise that there is no such thing as the Baptist Church. Each individual local Church manages its own affairs, and no outside body can decide how it should be governed.

But there are voluntary agencies which link Churches together – such as *The Baptist Union of Great Britain and Ireland*, formed in 1812. And there is a world-wide fellowship of Baptist Churches called the *Baptist World Alliance*.

Baby baptism 'a superstition'

The vicar of Eaton Socon parish at St. Neots, the Rev. John Heffer, believes the only way to get rid of the "superstitious nonsense" concerning baptism is to stop baptising infants.

"If the God and Father of our Lord Jesus Christ demands three drops of water sprinkled on the forehead before He will consider saving one of His children, then I must have been reading the Bible upside down all my life. I believe that the only way to get rid of this superstitious nonsense is to stop baptising infants—but who will listen to me?" the vicar adds.

Writing in the "News of the Churches" journal he says that superstition surrounds infant baptism to such an extent that many wondered if it was right to baptise anyone until they had reached an age when they could understand and make their own choice. Thus baptism and confirmation would come together.

"Whoever could believe that a baby who dies unbaptised would be consigned by Almighty God to eternal damnation?" asks Mr. Heffer.

From The Cambridge Evening News, Tuesday, 5 August 1975.

Think about . . .

This Church of England vicar believes in the baptism of both adult Christians and their children; but he says that the meaning of infant baptism is so often misunderstood that perhaps it would be better to keep baptism for adults only. Do you agree? What 'superstitious nonsense' concerning baptism does he reject?

2

Dangerous Revolutionaries

It is hard to imagine the respectable people who attend a Baptist Church as being enemies of the State. Yet that is how Baptists were once regarded. In some parts of the world they are *still* considered 'dangerous revolutionaries'.

The first Baptists were called Anabaptists (re-baptisers) because they rebaptised adult believers who had already been baptised as infants. These first Baptists were well-to-do citizens of Zurich in Switzerland. When they went to see Martin Luther, the great German Reformer, 450 years ago he was alarmed at some of their ideas. They not only held that none but saints (believing Christians) should be in the Church; they held that the state was in no sense a Christian institution and believing Christians should play no part in it. Let the sinners be the rulers and punish other sinners! Luther realised that these beliefs could undermine the whole of society – Church, state, and government. So in 1530 he said that such scamps should be silenced or sent to the hangman!

In England, people with similar views fared little better. Many were fined, imprisoned, and beaten.

Some fled by ship at night, risking betrayal and arrest. They settled at Amsterdam and Leiden in Holland. Eventually some sailed to North America where they helped to establish new colonies.

Those who stayed in England were regarded as law-breakers if they did not attend worship at the parish church. On 12 November 1660, John Bunyan of Bedford was arrested and put in prison because he had stayed away from his local parish church and persisted in preaching at farmhouses and wayside chapels in the surrounding countryside. When offered his freedom if he would give up this unlawful preaching, he said in effect that he would rather stay in prison until the moss grew on his eyebrows than go against his conscience. Altogether he spent some twelve years in jail, where he wrote his famous book *Pilgrim's Progress*, while his blind daughter Mary sold shoe-laces outside the prison to raise money for the rest of the family.

All that seems a long time ago, and the rights for which Free Churchmen fought three centuries ago are now taken for granted in most civilised countries. There is now very much more freedom of thought within the Church of England than was possible in Bunyan's day, while variations in belief and interpretation of the Bible now cause the Free Churches difficulties of their own.

However, there are still some parts of the world where for very different reasons, man's basic right to liberty of conscience is denied.

In 1965 a nineteen-year-old girl from Leningrad was put in prison for distributing an 'unofficial religious letter'. Some time before, she had written out some copies of her own New Year's poem, and had given them to passers-by. But when a hostile journalist called Valen Kuzin got hold of a copy, he wrote an article in the Russian young people's newspaper *Smena* accusing her of going to illegal meetings and publishing unofficial literature. He believed her propaganda about life after death undermined Communist efforts to improve life here on earth.

Being a spirited person, Aida decided to answer back. But because no newspaper would print her 4000 word reply, she typed and distributed her own copies once more.

Aida Skripnikova

She pointed out that while her critic Valen was free to meet anybody he wished, the Authorities would not recognise her Church as an official one, so all her meetings were bound to be 'illegal'.

Moreover, because Christian young people in Russia were not allowed to have their own newspaper, as other young people were, she was forced to send out her article as an 'unofficial religious letter'.

She said that competing with Valen was like running a race against him after he had tied both her legs together!

Her vigorous article got her into trouble right away. And when she said at her trial: 'Believers cannot promise to fulfill a law which forbids them to talk about God, and bans parents from bringing up their children in the faith', imprisonment was inevitable.

Most of the half million members of the *All-Union Council of Evangelical Christians – Baptists* in Russia today are relatively free from harassment. But that has not always been the case either before or since the Revolution in 1917. The fine preaching, stirring singing, and deeply moving Communion services of the crowded Baptist Churches in the Soviet Union have impressed numerous visitors from the West.

But there are many Christians like Aida who believe that the State interferes too much with the internal affairs of the Churches, and that many government regulations about religion are too restrictive. When these *Reform Baptists* go on to claim complete freedom of religion, which they consider to be their right, they experience considerable hardship.

After spending a year in prison, Aida continued to be ridiculed, harassed, and interrogated. From 1968 to 1971 she served a further sentence in the Potma Prison Complex.

At her trial she said: 'I am not a heroine. I love freedom and would very much like to be free now with my family and friends. But I cannot buy freedom at *any* price, I don't want to act against my conscience. I love freedom; but what good is freedom to me if I cannot call God my Father? . . . The knowledge that my soul and thoughts are free encourages and strengthens me.'

Today this trained laboratory technician is out of prison and employed as an announcer at a railway station near Leningrad.

Think about . . .

The story of the anabaptists mentioned at the beginning of this chapter can be read in *The Penguin History of Christianity* by Roland Bainton, Vol. 2 pp. 133–135.

The life and experiences of John Bunyan: there is a short biography for children: *To Be A Pilgrim* by Joyce Reason (Lutterworth Press). The B.B.C. produce an LP of readings from his *Pilgrim's Progress* (RESR 1). Modern versions of his story are available, and six C.P.A.S. filmstrips of it can be hired from the Scripture Union, Wigmore Street, London W.1.

Explore the differences between the Official and Reform Baptists in the Soviet Union. Aida's story is told in *Faith on Trial in Russia* by Michael Bourdeaux (a Hodder & Stoughton paperback), and in *Aida of Leningrad* published by Mowbrays. Dr E. A. Payne has written a useful book about the Official Baptists, *Out of Great Tribulation* (Baptist Publications) – though its spelling of Russian names is sometimes rather eccentric! From time to time there are useful articles on the situation in the *Baptist Times* which comes out each Thursday. Material produced by *The Centre for the Study of Religion and Communism* at Keston College, Kent BR2 6BA, is always up to date and most reliable. See too *Young Christians in Russia* by Michael Bourdeaux and Katharine Murray (Lakeland). For advanced students, Trevor Beeson's *Discretion and Valour* (Fontana) gives an accurate assessment of the present situation.

3

A Free Church in a Free State

THE NATIONAL CHURCH   In 1974 Dr Michael Ramsay, the Archbishop of Canterbury, retired, and on the advice of her Prime Minister, the Queen appointed Dr Donald Coggan to be his successor.

This method of choosing archbishops and bishops has been going on for centuries. As our coins indicate, the Queen is *F.D.* or *Fid. Def.* – 'Defender of the Faith': she is the recognised head of the Church of England.

This means that her bishops sit in the House of Lords and have some say in what laws are passed by Parliament, and Christian ideas help to influence the way people think and act. Leading Churchmen conduct royal weddings, coronations and state funerals. Throughout our long history, the Church has helped to unite the nation – especially in times of difficulty.

But not everybody is happy with this situation. Perhaps there is no problem about a 'National' Church when the reigning monarch is a convinced Christian, and when most people accept the Christian way of life. But who can say for how long the nation will remain 'Christian'? At the present time many people think it is unfair that the Christian Church should have such a prominent part in our way of life when it no longer appears to have the support of most people in Britain. They feel it is time the Church had less say in politics, education, and public morals.

A FREE CHURCH   Along with other Christian groups – some of which have now come together in the United Reformed Church – Baptists were uneasy about the state ruling the 'National' ('Established') Church when they first began.

From their study of the Bible, they believed that the Church should be separate from the state, and that while Christians should 'render to Caesar (the state) what belongs to Caesar', it should render to God alone what belongs to God (Matt. 22:21, Rom. 13:1, Acts 4:19).

They maintained that Christian people must always support the state when it is just. But their first loyalty is to Jesus Christ, and they must be free to resist the state when it acts unjustly.

As a result, Baptists formed separate churches where believing people, who were willing to be guided by the teaching of Jesus in the Bible, could study and worship together without state control. Theirs were 'Free' Churches as opposed to the Established Church.

TENSIONS   It is easy to see why Baptists and other Free Church-men were so unpopular when they put these ideas into practice nearly 400 years ago. The authorities were shocked by what they considered to be disloyalty both to the state and to the reigning monarch of the time – especially as many Baptists had fought in Oliver Cromwell's army against Charles I. They feared that if this attitude spread to other laws besides religious ones, there would be anarchy.

When a group of *extreme* re-baptisers (or 'anabaptists' as they were called) took over the town of Münster in Germany for a short time in the sixteenth century, there was a total breakdown of law and order. What if that should happen in England too?

But as time has gone on, the sharp edges of this old debate have become blunted. Free Churches have shown that they have a *positive* role to play in society. The Anglican Church is itself much freer from Parliament's control than was once the case. And the state accepts the fact that in certain circumstances people must be free to follow their own consciences.

The same is not yet true of certain Communist countries, however. Because they believe that everything in the state should be under the control of the state, Communists are suspicious of any group of people wanting to be completely independent. They fear that people opposed to some Communist ideas might undermine the state if they were allowed too much freedom. And because they believe that ultimately their atheistic system will completely replace religion, they are embarrassed when so many of their people let it be known that they are Christians.

So they try to keep down the number of religious people by imposing restrictions, refusing to register too many places of worship, and by making life difficult for people like Aida Skripnikova.

A group of Reform Baptists worshipping in the woods outside Leningrad. Aida has her back to the camera.

Think about . . .

If the Church should be separate from the state, as Baptists claim, is it right for Baptists to teach religion in state schools, accept appointments as hospital chaplains, or receive grants to train for the Baptist ministry? (Always remembering that Baptists should dutifully pay their rates and taxes, of course!) Incidentally, can you think of any other groups within society which also claim the right to be free from state control? Is it possible for any body of people to be *totally* independent of government action?

4

Every Member Matters

BEING INVOLVED   One result of being a Free Church is that Baptists have to be responsible for their own affairs. Parish churches may make public appeals for financial help to repair the roof, renovate the stone work, or replace the bells. But most Baptists feel they should not look to the community at large for this sort of help. It is their *own* responsibility.

It is true that churches in the Baptist Union may be able to claim help from central funds to support a Minister or put up a building. But even when a congregation finds it necessary to have this sort of assistance, its members are usually only too anxious to become financially independent as soon as possible.

This means that most Baptist churches with a membership of 100 or less cannot afford luxurious amenities – even if they were to want them! In fact a small 'tin chapel' in the back street of some city slum may represent many years of hard work and sacrificial giving on the part of a small Baptist congregation in that area.

It also means that every member of a Baptist church has to pull his weight and play his part – not only to raise money but to sustain the work of the church in every department. Church work is team work.

Some firms in Britain are only just getting used to the idea of 'industrial democracy' where the workers are allowed a share in making decisions and managing the company. But Baptists have been practising this sort of power-sharing for nearly four centuries. In fact, together with other Free Churches, they helped to pioneer this kind of democracy in the West.

But of course it is not merely 'power-sharing' or 'democracy' which they practise. Baptists believe that when they meet together as a group of Christians, Christ himself is present with them and makes his will known to them as they pray, debate, and act.

GETTING ORGANISED   Once a month – or quarterly, in some cases – the members of a local Baptist church attend a Church Meeting at which decisions about the church's life and work are made. The members do not merely *go* to church: they *are* the church; and it is their responsibility to carry on the work of God in their locality.

Before the meeting, the Church Secretary draws up an agenda with a list of topics to be discussed. Afterwards he, or an assistant, writes summaries of the discussions held and the decisions made. These summaries are known as 'minutes'.

Decisions are usually reached by members voting on resolutions which have been proposed and seconded in the proper way. But because voting can sometimes be divisive, as well as unnecessary, some churches try to reach agreement by discussion alone rather than by a 'show of hands', if at all possible.

Clearly the members cannot be involved in *all* the day-to-day business of running the church, so 'deacons' are appointed to act on their behalf. The word 'deacon' simply means 'someone who serves', and it comes from the New Testament (Acts 6:1–6). The deacons are expected to live good lives, set an example to the rest of the church, and give leadership (I Tim. 3:8–13). And as in New Testament times, women as well as men may be chosen as deacons (Rom. 16:1).

In some Baptist churches, a further group of officers known as

'Elders' are appointed. They may not necessarily be older people, as their title might suggest. But they are expected to be mature Christians who will support the Minister in his work, visit any members who might be in special difficulty, and give advice.

If possible, the Church invites a man or woman to become its full-time Minister. As a rule, the Minister has been trained at one of the Baptist Theological Colleges. But sometimes a church may 'call' someone who has never received any special training. When that happens, he or she usually follows a course of study recommended by the Baptist Union before becoming officially recognised as an 'accredited' Minister.

A church which is unable to support a Minister may join up with one or more Baptist churches in the area and share the services of an ordained Minister with them.

Roger Pearse, an accredited Supplementary Minister, earns his living in the Probation and After-care Service.

He is also part of the team of ministers working on a GLC overspill housing estate in Bletchley.

24

In some cases, smaller churches may secure the services of a man or woman who has received special training for the Ministry, but who spends most of his or her time in some other occupation such as teaching or the social services. This is sometimes known as the 'Supplementary Ministry'.

Very many Baptist churches in villages rely almost entirely on the services of lay preachers who earn their living in the normal way, but devote many hours of their own time to study, preparation, and preaching.

It goes without saying that the Church Secretary carries a lot of responsibility. He not only deals with all the correspondence; he acts as go-between and adviser, listening to every point of view, keeping the congregation informed, and aiding the Minister in his work.

The Treasurer takes care of the offerings. He pays bills on behalf of the congregation. He gives advice about all the Church's financial affairs. He handles complicated matters like insurance, tax, rates and covenants. And once a year he presents a balance sheet to the members, showing what money has come in, and how much has gone out.

Although names have been altered and figures simplified, the following is an actual balance sheet presented to the members of a Baptist Church in January 1974. It should be pointed out that this represents the work of 135 members, that the Minister's 'stipend' (not salary) was augmented by additional fees from other sources and did not include the cost of a Manse provided for him rent-free and rate-free, and that the 'subscriptions and donations' listed in the 'payments' column were for causes like:

Christian Aid, a school for the handicapped, holiday club for children, children's home, the West Ham Central Mission, the Sailors' Society, two Baptist Colleges, the Bible Society, the Baptist Union, Earl Haig Fund, the local Council of Churches, a school for missionaries' children, Christian Education Council, Benevolent Fund, etc.

PARK VIEW BAPTIST CHURCH BARTON WELLS

Balance Sheet as at 31.12.73

1972	Receipts	1973	1972	Payments	1973
193.90	Balance brought forward	174.10	1280.00	Minister's stipend	1355.00
2542.82	Weekly offerings	2775.86	284.91	Minister's expenses, insurance etc.	298.00
216.00	Covenanted subscriptions	216.00	108.68	Stationery, printing,advertising	152.36
123.17	Donations	96.74	30.00	Organist	30.00
18.30	Hire of hall	18.22	231.70	Light and heat	344.90
67.35	Canteen proceeds	78.51	238.59	Rates, insurance, maintenance	194.30
23.57	Manse trust fund	23.57	98.99	Newsletters	89.23
405.48	Donations received for	559.92	35.35	Sunday School expenses	65.54
	Missionary Society and		107.15	Boiler maintenance	18.70
	other causes		53.26	Canteen	62.54
			82.70	Subscriptions and donations	141.30
			285.00	Cleaning	267.90
			50.00	Church Fellowship Fund	50.00
3590.59		3942.92	18.75	Purchase of Bibles	37.50
			19.00	Presentations	4.30
			87.37	Postages, telephone, pulpit supply	105.85
			32.51	Other expenses	27.36
			254.45	Baptist Missionary Society	285.43
	Organ fund	52.57	118.07	Home Mission Fund	134.30
				Transfer to Reserve fund	100.00
	Reserve account	1790.77	174.10	Balance at bank	178.50
			3590.59		3942.92

A.R.Cooper Esq., A.S.B.I.
Hon. Treasurer 2.1.74

Audited and found correct
A.Smith
P.Baker

From the figures provided here, how much money did each member give each week on average? How much was given to causes outside the local Church, e.g. through subscriptions and donations, as well as through contributions to the Baptist Missionary Society and the Home Mission Fund (which help needier Baptist Churches)? What percentage of the total expenditure of the Church does this amount represent? Do you think this is a fair percentage? It should be pointed out that these figures have increased considerably each year since 1974.

5

What Does the Scripture Say?

Most young people look forward to the day when they can be free to manage their own lives, make their own decisions, and stand on their own feet. They know that this is the only way to become mature.

But freedom is useless, even dangerous, unless it is freedom *for* something. We are free to choose who or what we will *serve*. If we say we will serve nobody – that we will please ourselves – that is a way of saying we choose to serve our impulses, our lower nature.

Christians believe that true liberty is choosing to serve God and to do what pleases him. For Baptists, and for many other Christians, that means getting to know the Bible. There are other ways in which men can be aware of God's will for their lives, but it is supremely by reading the Bible that God's intentions are understood.

There is no final agreement among Baptists about how the Bible should be regarded. Some believe that every syllable of it was inspired by God. Others maintain that while the Bible contained God's word for the men and women who lived at the time when its various books were first written, we ourselves must get behind its out-dated words and ideas to discover how it applies to us today. Perhaps most Baptists take up a position midway between these two points of view.

Again there are differences of view among Baptists on what the Bible actually teaches about important topics. The earliest strand of Baptist life believed that all men everywhere can and should respond to the love of God which is shown to us in Jesus Christ. They were known as the *General Baptists*, among whom were John Smith, who founded the first English Baptist church while living in Holland with other religious exiles; and Thomas Helwys, his colleague, who later founded the first known Baptist church in London.

But almost from the start there was another section of the movement which believed that while God is active everywhere throughout his universe, only those he has chosen and called can respond to him. These were known as *Particular Baptists* because they maintained that the death of Christ was only for a particular people: those destined to believe in him.

Both outlooks are still represented in churches which belong to the Baptist Union. There is also a denomination of some 700 churches known as the *Strict and Particular Baptists* which remains separate from the Baptist Union.

Yet while Baptists are rather reluctant to define their attitude towards the Bible more precisely, all are agreed that the Bible must be central to what they believe. Having no binding statements of faith at the present time – as previous generations of Baptists had – they cling to the Bible as their one rule of faith and conduct. And they believe with John Robinson, Minister of the Church in Holland, to which Smith and Helwys belonged, that 'the Lord hath yet more light and truth to break forth from His word'.

It was their understanding of the Bible which led Baptists to insist that the Church should be separate from the state. And it was through their study of the Bible that they came to accept that particular form of baptism which is their distinctive feature now.

This means that Baptists have always emphasised biblical

study. Overseas, Baptist missionaries like William Carey in India, and W. Holman Bentley in Zaire, made a great contribution to the churches they helped to bring into being, by translating the Bible into local languages. In Britain, Baptist scholars like L. H. Brockington, R. L. Child, A. R. Johnson, E. A. Payne, T. H. Robinson, and H. H. Rowley, helped to produce the New English Bible. The American Baptist, Dr Kenneth Taylor, has helped thousands of young people discover the Bible for themselves through his up-to-date version *The Living Bible*.

It also means that the Bible has normally played an important part in Baptist church services. There are some Baptist churches which have a fairly elaborate form of service. But as a rule, most services for worship in Baptist churches are very simple and straightforward. They usually consist of a number of hymns interspersed with readings, prayers and notices. Then as the

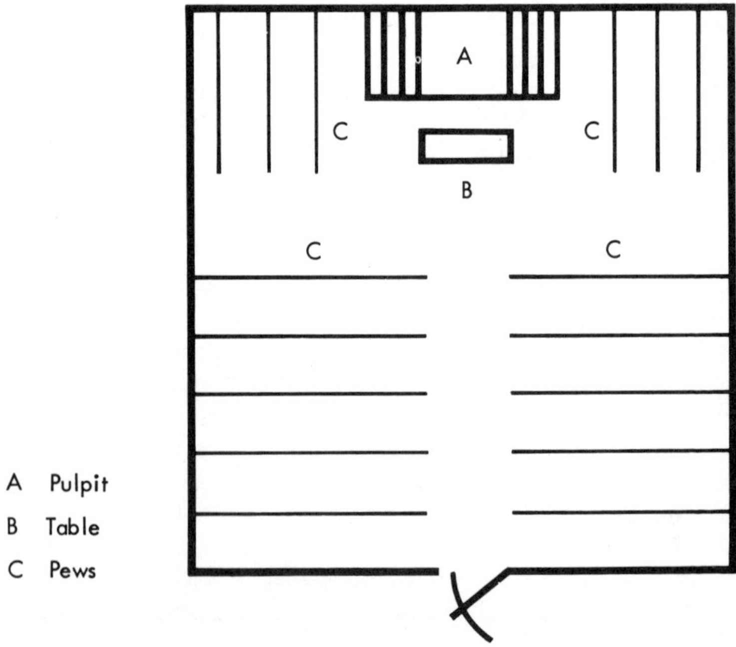

A Pulpit

B Table

C Pews

A typical early meeting-house.

climax to the service, the Bible is explained and applied to the lives of people in the congregation.

In the first Baptist Meeting-houses, the pulpit was placed in the very centre, in front of the congregation, with all seats facing it, to show how important it was for the people to hear God's words. And this was the pattern followed when huge 'Tabernacles' were built, with elaborate pulpits high above the congregation like thrones from which great preachers reigned!

Then in the nineteenth century a few Baptist Churches were built as much like the typical Anglican Church as possible, to give a sense of stateliness and dignity to the worship service.

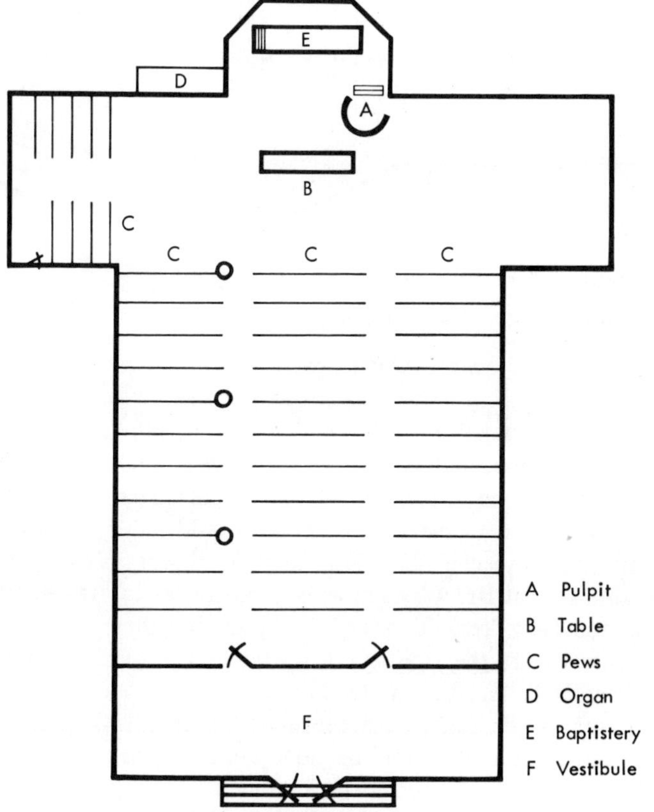

A nineteenth-century church.

31

When that happened, the pulpit was often placed to one side of the Church, with the Communion table, and sometimes the baptistery, in the centre.

But more recently, considerable thought has been given to the whole question of Baptist Church architecture, and some interesting designs have been produced, placing pulpit, communion table, and open baptistery, as centrally as possible.

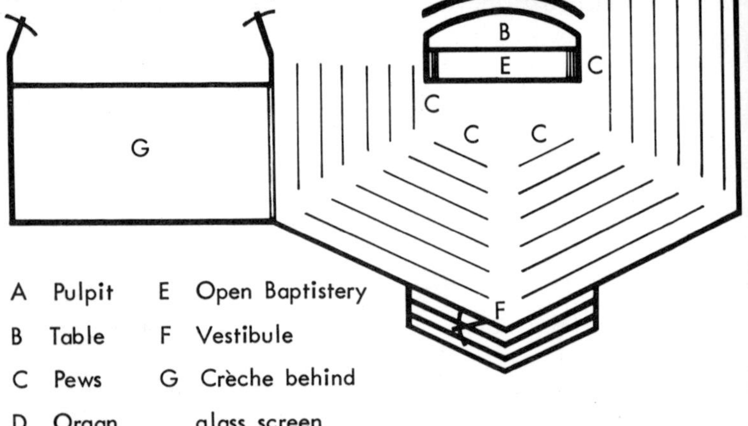

A   Pulpit   E   Open Baptistery

B   Table   F   Vestibule

C   Pews   G   Crèche behind

D   Organ   glass screen

A modern church.

In the days before radio and television, pulpit oratory was a great attraction, and Baptists, with their emphasis on the Bible, produced a long succession of power preachers. If one were to make a very long list indeed, many would still be omitted. But some are of special note. For example, Robert Hall's preaching in churches at Bristol, Cambridge and Leicester, was so effective that the New York Times said of him that there was no one in Britain whom the politicians feared and respected more than Robert Hall. He died in 1831.

Later in the nineteenth century, Alexander MacLaren made the Bible come alive for the huge congregations in Manchester which heard him preach every Sunday.

At the same time, John Clifford of Nottingham built up a

thriving church in West London through his passionate preaching and by daring to go to prison for his beliefs.

In 1854, a mile or so from the Kennington Oval, a young twenty-year-old Essex lad started with a congregation of two

Dr John Clifford: from a portrait in Baptist Church House.

hundred and within a few years was preaching to congregations of 6000 every Sunday. During thirty-eight years at the Metropolitan Tabernacle, C. H. Spurgeon founded numerous churches and Mission Halls, opened almshouses and orphanages, established a Theological College which still flourishes, and received 14 691 people into the membership of the Tabernacle. The sermons he preached are still being published a century later. Kenneth Slack describes him as 'possibly the greatest natural genius of the pulpit that England has produced . . . he was also a great entertainer, using every artifice of wit, humour, ingenuity and dramatic daring to drive home his message.' (*The British Churches Today* SCM 1961)

In our own day, the American evangelist, Dr Billy Graham, has probably preached to more people than any other preacher in history. Hiring exhibition halls, sports arenas, and public parks – often for weeks on end – and by using modern media such as radio, film, and television most effectively, this dynamic Baptist Minister has shown a remarkable ability to attract vast numbers of people to his crusades, and to persuade many thousands to make 'a decision for Christ'.

Think about . . .

Investigate the life and history of your local Baptist church. Describe its organisation, and discuss the architecture of its place of worship. Its officers will be only too pleased to give you all the help they can, and the following small booklets from Baptist Publications (4 Southampton Row, London WC1B 4AB) will give useful background information: *Meet the Family* (10p) and *Who are the Baptists?* (4p) by W. W. Bottoms; *What is a Baptist Church?* by L. R. Floyd (5p); *Baptist Places of Worship* by G. W. Rusling (5p); and *British Baptists Today* by D. S. Russell (8p).

Write a short biography of any outstanding Baptist who has lived in your area. Your local library will be able to supply you with valuable information. The library may also be able to obtain a copy of A. S. Clement's *Baptists Who Made History* (London 1955) which was specially written for young people. For reference purposes, more advanced books like: *A History of the Baptists* by Robert G. Torbet (London 1966), *The Baptist Union: A Short History* by E. A. Payne (London 1959), or *British Baptists* by D. M. Himbury, will be useful. *An Introduction to the Baptists* by Erroll Hulse (75p from Carey Publications, Haywards Heath, Sussex) tends to be rather scrappy, but it has some interesting line drawings and includes useful sketches of many Calvinistic Baptists sometimes ignored by other books. It should be borne in mind that because of inflation the prices mentioned here are likely to be increased from time to time.

6

Buried
to
Live Again

Water is one of life's most important commodities. It irrigates the soil, nurtures the crops, cleanses impurities, and slakes our thirst. Without it we would die.

Small wonder that most religions therefore regard water as a powerful symbol. In Derbyshire, villagers decorate their wells each year with biblical pictures made from flower petals. In India, pilgrims often trek hundreds of miles to bathe in the sacred waters of the Ganges.

Water holds an important place in the Jewish religion. Converts are baptised, and meals are accompanied by ritual washings and prayers. The gospels tell of John the Baptist calling men to repent and begin a new life by coming to be baptised in the River Jordan. They also tell how Jesus shared in this baptism, and immediately afterwards went off into the desert to think out the new life to which he felt called as he came up out of the water (Mark 1:4–13). Later they tell how Jesus regarded his own suffering and death as a 'baptism' (Mark 10:38–39, Luke 12:50).

The early Church adopted the practice of baptising converts in obedience to the instructions Jesus had given to his disciples (Matthew 28:19–20), and they explained the meaning of this rite in many ways:

- washing away the old life,
- purifying the mind and conscience,
- becoming a member of the Body which has Christ as its head,
- crossing the Red Sea to enter the promised land,
- being carried to safety as in Noah's Ark,
- putting on Christ, like new clothes,
- being buried to live again in a new age.

It was through studying the importance of baptism to the early Church that Baptists laid so much stress on the practice which has given them their name.

Many branches of the Christian Church have felt it right to baptise children in their infancy, especially in view of the welcome Jesus had given to little children (e.g. Mark 10:13–16). But Baptists insist that the New Testament associates baptism with a person's own faith in Jesus; and as very small children are not old enough to believe for themselves, baptism should be withheld until the child can make his or her own decision.

This is a very complicated subject, and some would say that by linking baptism with a person's faith in this way Baptists obscure the fact that baptism stands more for what God does for us than for what we do for him. And just as God loved us before ever we were conscious of that love, so too His gift of the Holy Spirit in baptism should be made available to us from the very beginning – whether we are old enough to experience faith for ourselves or not.

The student will need to look up references to baptism in the New Testament to make up his or her own mind on the question. But there is no doubt that in the first century baptism normally marked the start of a man's commitment to Jesus Christ. (See the references at the end of this chapter.)

The Book of Acts tells how 3000 people received baptism when Peter explained the Good News to them (Acts 2:41). Down in the Gaza Strip, an eminent politician from Ethiopia stepped down into the water to be baptised (Acts 8:38). The converted rabbi, Saul of Tarsus, was baptised as a Christian in Straight Street, Damascus (Acts 9:17–19).

When John Smith baptised himself and his friends at Amsterdam in the early 1600's, he did so by pouring water over the head. (The practice is called 'affusion'.) But later Baptists decided that probably in New Testament times the whole person was plunged under the water. So, making use of any pond, river, or stream nearby, they began to baptise converts by complete immersion.

John Bunyan was baptised in the River Ouse at Bedford. William Carey, founder of the Baptist Missionary Society, braved the waters of the River Nene at six o'clock in the morning on the first Sunday of October 1783. In May 1850, the fifteen-year-old Charles Spurgeon walked eight miles from Newmarket to Isleham Ferry to be baptised in the River Lark.

From time to time Baptists still make use of rivers or seas in this way. But most Baptist churches now have a baptistery built into the floor of the Church. In older buildings, the baptistery may be covered over when not in use. But increasingly there is a tendency to build baptisteries which can be kept open for all to see.

It is a great day when the pool comes into use. The candidate approaches the Minister some weeks before and requests baptism. The Minister questions the candidate to make sure he has made a personal commitment to Jesus Christ and understands a little of what it means to follow him. Quite often a number of baptismal classes for instruction are arranged. In some churches one or two visitors are appointed to meet the candidate and to report back to the church, especially if he or she has also asked to be accepted as a member of the church.

Then comes the long-awaited day when the candidate is to confess his or her faith in Christ. If the candidate is a girl, she will be dressed in a special white baptismal gown. If a boy, he will come dressed in shirt and flannels.

There will be a sense of 'occasion' in the service, and the Minister will normally be on his guard against letting the

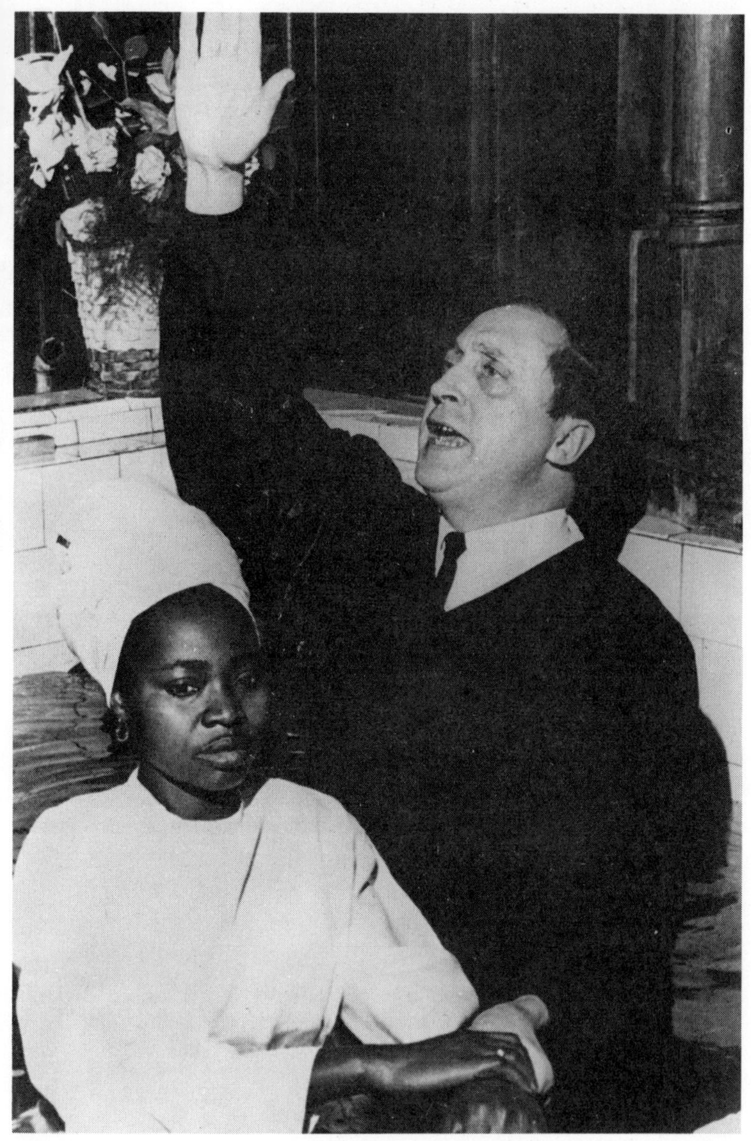

*Revd Mikhail Zhidkov of Moscow Baptist Church baptising
Miss Diaomadji of Chad on 2 August 1973.*

atmosphere become too emotional. There will be the usual hymns, prayers, readings, and sermon. Then during the hymn before the ceremony, the Minister will leave the church and don his special waders, before returning to the service, and descending the steps leading down into the baptistery.

In many churches, the candidate is expected to stand by the pool and to give some statement about how he or she came to faith in Christ. Then, once the candidate has entered the water, the Minister pronounces his or her name, and 'on profession of faith' plunges the candidate beneath the waters, baptising him or her 'into the name of the Father, the Son, and the Holy Spirit'. The congregation sings a hymn of faith and dedication, while the candidate leaves the baptistery and makes for the dressing room.

It goes without saying that if the person concerned is too old or ill to be baptised in this way, the baptism will be by affusion. But it is not unusual for disabled people to ask for immersion.

In churches belonging to the *Old Baptist Union* (as in most Russian Baptist churches) the minister also 'lays hands' on the baptismal candidates (Acts 8:17). But this is not generally practised in other Baptist churches at present.

Quite often the baptismal service is followed by a short celebration of Holy Communion. The candidate returns to the congregation, the Elders and Deacons join the Minister at the Communion table, prayers of thanksgiving for the death of Christ are offered – usually by one or other of the officers, and then the Deacons distribute both bread and wine to all those members of the congregation who wish to participate.

It is not normally a rigid rule that people who are baptised as believers should then join a *Baptist* church. But it is usually pointed out that the New Testament links together belief, baptism, and church membership, so that the candidate will normally be expected to join one or other of the Christian churches in his locality.

DISCIPLESHIP What does baptism mean? It is hard to put into words. Baptism – like art and drama – needs to be experienced rather than explained. But clearly the New Testament teaches that baptism is a kind of death and resurrection. It marks the end of a man's old way of living, and the commencement of a totally new quality of life lived out in the company of all other Christians.

Looking at what the New Testament has to say about it, we see that baptism is a kind of *statement*. Although no words may be used, the ceremony speaks very clearly of the way Jesus died and rose again, and how a man needs to be made clean – not merely by allowing the water to wash away dirt from his body, but by being given a clear conscience (1 Peter 3:21).

Baptism is also an act of *commitment*. As he goes down into the water and comes up again, the candidate is identifying himself with Jesus Christ in his death and resurrection (Rom. 6:4). And just as the candidate has taken off his normal clothing and put on his special baptismal attire, so in behaviour and experience he has put off his old way of life, and put on a totally new kind of life altogether (Gal. 3:27).

Moreover a close study of the New Testament will show that baptism is also to be seen as a *gift*. It is a way of doing what God requires (Matthew 3:15). It is an opportunity to confess Jesus as Lord (Romans 10:9). It is the place where one may receive forgiveness of sins, and a means of receiving God's Holy Spirit into the life (Acts 2:38). It is also the gateway into membership of Christ's Church (1 Cor. 12:13).

The above comments about the Bible's teaching on baptism owe much to Dr. G. R. Beasley-Murray's book *Baptism in the New Testament* (Macmillan 1962).

If you would like to think further about this subject you will need to study the following, making use of a good commentary:

> Concerning children: Matt. 18:1–4, 1 Cor. 7:13–14
>
> The command to baptise: Matt. 28:16–20
>
> About the relationship between faith and baptism:
>
> Acts 22:16, 1 Peter 3:21 (cleansing)
>
> Gal. 3:27 (union with Christ)
>
> Gal. 2:20, Col. 2:10–13 (new life)
>
> Acts 2:37–38 (receiving the Holy Spirit)
>
> (but see also Acts 1:5, Acts 11:15–18)

The following small booklets may be obtained from Baptist Publications: *Seven Reasons for Believers Baptism* by F. B. Meyer (5p), *Invitation to Baptism* by R. E. O. White (18p), *Your Baptism* (10p) and *New Testament Teaching on Baptism* (18p) by S. F. Winward.

In place of 'Infant Baptism' many Baptist churches have a service of Infant Dedication in which parents thank God for their child and promise to bring it up as a Christian – with the help of the whole church.

Incidentally, it should be pointed out that in some 'open membership' Baptist churches, it is possible for members of other Free Churches which do not practise baptism of any kind (e.g. Salvation Army) to be accepted as full members. In such cases, therefore, it is possible to be a member of a Baptist church *without ever having been baptised*!

7

A Church
without
Walls

OUTREACH   Some years ago, the Baptists produced a small book for young people about *Baptists Who Made History*. Out of thirteen personalities described in its 136 pages, no less than *seven* were missionaries, – *eight* if you include Roger Williams, who not only established the first Baptist Church in America, but also befriended the Red Indians, learned their language, and explained the Christian faith to them.

That fact alone will give some idea of the prominence given by Baptists to missionary work. Indeed it was a Baptist – William Carey – who helped to spark off the extraordinary expansion of missionary activity among Protestant Christians over the past 200 years.

It began with Captain Cook's voyages! William Carey was so enthralled by the great explorer's discoveries, that he made a globe out of leather scraps in his shoe-repair shop at Moulton, so that he could plot the new territories being opened up in the Pacific.

He collected statistics about the new peoples described by Captain Cook, discovered all he could about their religious customs, and published a book which urged that Christian missionaries should go to these people as soon as possible.

Not all of his fellow Baptists were impressed by his arguments, but Carey was not the sort of person to be put off very easily. He had faced the disapproval of his own family when he suddenly turned Baptist in 1779. Now he was just as prepared to wear down the prejudice of his fellow Baptists against foreign missions.

By this time he had moved to Harvey Lane Baptist Church in Leicester where he was helping to build up a strong work. When he preached in Nottingham on 31 May 1792, he urged the congregation to 'expect great things from God, and attempt great things for God'. Then on 2 October of the same year, he and a group of like-minded people met together in Widow Wallis's little cottage at Kettering, and with a collection of gifts and promises amounting to *£13.2s.6d*, launched the world-wide work of the Baptist Missionary Society.

At the age of thirty-two he set sail for India. Originally he had intended going to the Islands of the South Pacific. But when he met an excitable and rather eccentric doctor called John Thomas, who was already working as a missionary in India, Carey decided to accompany him.

Like many a missionary before and since, Thomas turned out to be something of a law unto himself. But not only did he direct Carey to his life's work, he also succeeded in winning the very first convert of the B.M.S. after seven years' patient toil in Bengal: a man called Krishna Pal.

The list of Carey's achievements in India is considerable. He ran an indigo factory for several years, became Professor of Bengali, Marathi, and Sanskrit at Fort William Government College, and campaigned for social reforms in India.

When he was joined by Joshua Marshman from Hull, and William Ward from Derby, he went to live at Serampore, where he set up a printing press, built a paper mill, and published India's first newspaper.

In 1810 he founded the Serampore University, which is still a major institution for higher education for all of Asia. And between them, Carey and his colleagues translated the Bible in whole or part into thirty-five different languages and dialects (including the whole Bible in Chinese).

For many years, the three families – including Carey's sick wife – lived together in a Christian commune, sharing all their possessions.

It is sometimes claimed that missionary work was really an extension of Western Imperialism: that everywhere the soldiers went, the missionaries were sure to go. But in fact Carey faced considerable opposition from the British authorities in India at various times, and both he and his colleagues had to enter India under the protection of the Danish flag.

Carey may not have been the 'Father of Modern Missions' as some claim. Others, such as John Eliot, were in the field long before him. But this rural shoe-maker, schoolmaster, botanist, zoologist, and linguist from Northamptonshire, was able to inspire Christians of other Churches to set up societies for sending missionaries overseas.

In 1944 the Baptist Missionary Society placed a plaque to commemorate him in the Parish Church at Paulerspury, the village where Carey was born on 17 August 1761. Five years later, in 1949, a lectern was dedicated in his honour at Westminster Abbey.

PARTNERSHIP   For the most part, Baptists have tended to be independent and insular. It is true that from the beginning local churches have banded themselves into 'Associations'. And churches within the Baptist Union have the advice and help of Area Superintendents – especially in securing the services of a Minister. But Baptists can become so absorbed in the affairs of their local churches that wider claims can be overlooked.

However, William Carey gave his fellow Baptists a *world* vision, and now there must be very few Baptist churches which do not have a vital concern for the work of God all over the world.

As a rule, each local church appoints a Missionary Secretary who distributes magazines, collects subscriptions, arranges functions, and keeps members informed about missionary activity. Then each year, a number of missionaries home on 'furlough' (which is supposed to be a holiday!) descend on some town or city in a given area, and each Baptist church for miles around receives a visit from one or more of the missionaries for at least one of its Sunday services.

Women play an important part in Baptist church life. There are some ordained women Ministers, including a number who once belonged to a Baptist order of Deaconesses with special skills in social work service; and there are women Church Officers such as secretaries, treasurers and deacons. Most Baptist churches have at least one women's meeting each week: sometimes more. And besides giving help, cheer, and companionship to many busy or lonely women, the Baptist Women's League – or one of its sister organisations such as 'Young Wives' – does much to support missionary activity through sales of work, garden parties, and exhibitions, as well as by direct giving.

In the same way the Baptist Men's Movement support agricultural missionaries in developing countries, by raising money for their support and sending much needed machinery to them.

Many Baptist Sunday Schools also send money to B.M.S. schools and hospitals, while Young Peoples' organisations sponsor the usual walks, work-ins, and work-outs familiar to fund-raisers everywhere!

In 1973 Baptists of the United Kingdom raised more than half a million pounds to support some 450 missionaries at work in nine different countries of the world. In the same year, two great Baptist Conventions in the United States raised more than $30 000 000 between them for world-wide missionary work.

UNITY   There has been rather less enthusiasm among Baptists for Carey's idea of *coordinating* all missionary activity, however. He had hoped to hold a great International Conference for missionaries of all denominations at the Cape of Good Hope in 1810. But Andrew Fuller, the Secretary of the B.M.S., did not share Carey's outlook at this point, and the project fell through.

It was not until a century later, in 1910, that such a Conference was held – this time at Edinburgh; and although Baptists took their full part in the work of that conference, they have not all approved of the World Council of Churches which has arisen since that time.

On the whole, Baptists have tended to be suspicious of powerful church structures. They remember their own struggles in the past, and are not eager to give up the hard-won liberties they enjoy. Moreover, because each Baptist church is independent, it is not really possible for anyone to speak on behalf of all Baptists – even though they democratically elect a Baptist Union Council every year! So negotiations towards unity with other denominations are difficult, though various national Baptist Unions have voted to take part in discussions about unity.

But having said that, it is true to say that many leading Baptists feel church unity to be vitally important. The Baptist churches of North India have joined with other denominations to form the *United Church of North India* – where they now have their first Baptist bishop! In England, a number of Baptist churches and Ministers have helped to set up United churches in various localities – especially in new towns or on new housing estates. And outstanding leaders, such as Dr E. A. Payne, one time Secretary of the Baptist Union, hold positions of esteem and influence within the World Council of Churches.

Certainly, wherever there are evangelistic efforts aimed at reaching a whole community with the Christian message, Baptists are usually represented on the organising committees.

Select the life story of any one missionary described in *Baptists who made History* and study it in depth.

What difficulties did William Carey face in carrying out his mission? What methods did he use? And was he justified in trying to convert Hindus to the Christian faith? Carey's story is told in a number of books such as *Eagle Omnibus 3* (Edinburgh House Press), *How Christianity Spread in England* by R. W. Thomson – himself a Baptist (R.E.P.), and *Faith Looks Outward* in Longman's 'Developing World' series. Iris Clinton also tells it for young people in the Faith and Fame book: *Young Man in a Hurry*.

8

Let Freedom Reign!

RELIGIOUS LIBERTY Baptists are Protestants. Like Martin Luther they stress a man's personal relationship with God, and seek to follow Jesus as he is described in scripture.

This means that sometimes they have emphasised the *individual* too much. But they have also attempted to apply their faith to everyday life in society. And even their emphasis on the individual has had beneficial results for others.

Baptists believe that a man is not a Christian merely because he has been born into a 'Christian' country, but because he has believed for himself. Therefore, along with their sister churches, the Presbyterians and Congregationalists (now the United Reformed Church), as well as the Society of Friends, Baptists have challenged what seems to them a *tribal* view of religion, and have insisted that every man must be free to make his own choice in this area of human experience.

This stand has resulted in considerable suffering for them. John Smith, the Church of England lecturer from Lincoln, who founded the first English Baptist Church in Holland after meeting a group of anabaptists called Mennonites, died in exile. Others languished in jail. Numerous Baptists suffered loss of homes, livelihood, and status. It has only been within the last hundred years, for example, that nonconformists have been allowed to graduate from Cambridge and Oxford Universities.

Other Christians have taken up the torch of freedom, but Baptists are *still* involved in the struggle for religious liberty. A leading Rumanian Baptist, Iosef Ton, has protested against Government interference in his Church's affairs, and suffered considerable harassment as a result.

Some Baptists in Eastern Europe, much admired by Alexander Solzhenitzyn, the exiled Russian writer, campaign for religious freedom by breaking restrictive laws and by publicising their plight as widely as possible.

Others patiently carry on their work within the guidelines laid down by the Government, attracting young and old to the Christian faith by their fine Christian characters and by their vigorous church life.

It is easy to make heroes of either group of Baptists. But recent study has shown that it is unwise for those who live at a distance to pass judgments on the men and women who are actually involved in the struggle for religious freedom in countries where Communism holds sway.

SOCIAL SERVICE Nowadays most Governments recognise the need to care for the less fortunate members of society. But for centuries this was mostly the churches' responsibility, and Baptists, like other Christians, have played their part in this 'caring' ministry.

Overseas they have opened schools and hospitals, developed communities which were once primitive, and championed the cause of social justice. In India, William Carey protested against the Hindu custom of Sati, which required widows to burn themselves to death on the husband's funeral pyre; eventually the practice was banned by law.

At home, Baptists have been involved in political movements aimed at fighting injustice and raising living standards. When a

Sunderland-born young Minister, R. Rowntree Clifford, arrived at the Barking Road Baptist Tabernacle, East London, in 1897, he found that several deacons had resigned, many members had left, and the Church was in debt. But an old tailor at Chelmsford who used to donate £5 out of the £30 he earned each year to worthy causes, heard of the young man's struggles, and gave him a total of £18 towards his work. This generous act set off a chain reaction, and people were prompted to give more, until the debt was cleared, and new premises were built.

When unemployment soared, Rowntree Clifford and Sister Hettie – who was later to be his wife – gathered a team of dedicated workers, and provided food, shelter, and work on the premises of the West Ham Central Mission (as the Church is now called).

At one time the membership of the Mission reached 2485. And although war scattered the congregation, some forty full time workers are still involved in its work of caring for young and old, under the leadership of Revd Stanley Turl J.P., President of the Baptist Union in 1975; and future social workers receive valuable training on the Mission's premises.

Revd Stanley Turl in harmony with two of his very young people.

CIVIL RIGHTS Two names stand out as shining examples of
Baptist involvement in the cause of civil rights.

William Knibb (1803–1845) came from the town of Kettering
in Northamptonshire. When his older brother Thomas died after
only a few weeks as a missionary in Kingston, Jamaica, twenty-
year-old William volunteered to take his place.

He arrived with his new bride Mary in 1825, took over his
brother's school, raised money to replace its outworn equipment,
and set about building a new extension.

Before long he became involved in the fight to end slavery.
When harsh laws forbade slaves to marry, preach, or seek their

William Knibb

52

freedom, and when the Planters and other slave-owners refused to obey the British law which banned the sale of slaves, William preached about the situation fearlessly.

He urged the slaves not to strike or rebel. Yet when the sugar works went up in flames on 27 December 1832, he was held responsible, and flung into jail. It was 14 February before he was formally discharged after an independent inquiry had found him innocent. Even then, assassins visited his home intent on ending his life.

Knibb's fellow missionaries decided to send him home to England to speak on behalf of the 800 000 slaves in the West Indies. Wherever he went, crowds gathered to hear his impassioned speeches condemning the lies and lawlessness of the Planters. Church leaders tried to get him to moderate his language, but he would not be silenced, and as Dr E. A. Payne has said 'the meetings Knibb addressed in all parts of the country . . . and his evidence before committees of both Houses of Parliament, contributed materially to the ending of slavery in the British colonies'.

In more recent times, the famous negro Baptist Minister, Dr Martin Luther King, campaigned for full civil rights for the descendants of former slaves in North America.

In August 1963 he addressed a crowd of 100 000 people at the Lincoln Memorial in Washington. His stirring speech outlined his dream of the day when the sons of former slaves and the sons of former slave owners would sit down together at the table of brotherhood; when his four little children would be judged not by the colour of their skin but by the content of their character; when freedom would reign from every mountainside in America; when 'all of God's children, black men and white men, Jews and Gentiles, Protestants and Catholics, will be able to join hands and sing in the words of the old negro spiritual: "Free at last, free at last, thank God Almighty, we are free at last" '.

His movement did much to bring about greater freedom and equality for the twenty million coloured people in the United States. He died on 4 April 1968, shot while standing on the balcony of a hotel in Memphis, Tennessee.

Think about . . .

Find out all you can about the Congregationalists
and Presbyterians. (See the companion booklet on the
United Reformed Church in this series.) Who were
the Mennonites? – They are still quite strong in parts
of Europe and the U.S.A. In the early eighteenth
century many General Baptists ceased to believe that
Jesus was God as well as man, and became Unitarians.
See what you can discover about the present day
Unitarians. *The Oxford Dictionary of the Christian
Church* will help.

Who were the Pilgrim Fathers and what did they
achieve? How does their story relate to that of the
Baptists? In addition to various school books contain-
ing the story of the Pilgrim Fathers, there is an
excellent Jackdaw folder on the topic. See too the
story of Roger Williams, who protested that the white
settlers in America often denied to others the freedom
they claimed for themselves.

'Martin Luther King's non-violent protest was a
noble failure'. Do you think this is true? His story is
told in *Christianity in Action Today* (Schofield and
Sims), as well as in Ian Birnie's *Four Working for
Humanity* (Edward Arnold). The Carwal soundstrip
The Dream of Martin Luther King gives the background to the racial conflict in America, and includes
a recording of Dr King's famous speech. While the
Fontana paperback *Strength to Love*, by Dr King
himself, sums up his philosophy most beautifully.

9

Yours Truly

The idea of 'freedom' has run like a thread through this account of *the Baptists*. But that is only one strand of the story. Baptist leaders have pointed out that just as the various members of a local Church belong together and form one body, so the many Churches of the Baptist denomination should covenant together as a unity. There must be inter-dependence as well as independence. Those who claim liberty should also display loyalty, mutual respect, and a strong sense of responsibility.

The Baptist Union has attempted to give expression to this sense of 'togetherness' on a national level – just as the Baptist World Alliance links together as many Baptist bodies as possible throughout the world.

But it would not be right to ignore the fact that differences of belief have sometimes made it very difficult for sincere Baptists to join together in this way. So while I have described those Churches which belong to the Baptist Union as being truly representative of *the Baptists*, I have tried to remember that a considerable number of Baptists are at present outside its membership.

I am most grateful to the Staff at Baptist Church House for much help and advice, to Revd Michael Bordeaux M.A., B.D., for expert guidance concerning the situation in Eastern Europe, and to the secretaries of the Southern Baptist and American Baptist Conventions in the United States for a great deal of information.

However, it is only fair to all concerned to say that the views expressed here are entirely my own.

One should add, moreover, that Baptists represent only one regiment in the Christian army, and while I have stressed the points at which they *differ* from their fellow Christians, it is important to remember that there is much more that *unites* them to members of other denominations.

THE BAPTIST UNION DECLARATION OF PRINCIPLE

The basis of this union is:

1.   That our Lord and Saviour Jesus Christ, God manifest in the flesh, is the sole and absolute authority in all matters pertaining to faith and practice, as revealed in the Holy Scriptures, and that each Church has liberty, under the guidance of the Holy Spirit, to interpret and administer His Laws.

2.   That Christian Baptism is the immersion in water into the Name of the Father, the Son, and the Holy Ghost, of those who have professed repentance towards God and faith in our Lord Jesus Christ who 'died for our sins according to the Scriptures, was buried, and rose again the third day'.

3.   That it is the duty of every disciple to bear personal witness to the Gospel of Jesus Christ, and to take part in the evangelisation of the world.

Important Dates

1612	John Smith, who founded the first English Baptist Church while living in Holland, dies in exile. His friend, Thomas Helwys (1550–1616) founds the first Baptist Church on English soil at Spitalfields in London.
1639	Roger Williams (1600–1685) founds the first Baptist Church in America.
1662	The Act of Uniformity makes it illegal for Ministers with Free Church views to stay in the Church of England. More than 2000 such clergymen are therefore expelled.
1678	John Bunyan (1628–1688) publishes his *Pilgrim's Progress*.
1792	The Baptist Missionary Society is founded at the home of Mrs Beeby Wallis in Kettering on 2nd October by William Carey (1761–1834) and his friends. The first secretary is Andrew Fuller (1754–1815) whose life and writings have helped to make the Mission possible.
1812	The Baptist Union is founded at Carters Lane, London, on June 25.
1813	Adoniram Judson (1788–1850) starts work as a missionary in Burma.

1823	Johann Oncken (1800–1884) 'Father of the Continental Baptists' starts work in Germany.
1831	Death of Robert Hall (b. 1764).
1833	Slavery abolished throughout the British Empire. William Knibb (1803–1845) has played a large part in the abolition campaign by conducting numerous Public Meetings throughout Britain, and by giving evidence before Parliament for six days.
1854	The twenty-year-old Charles Haddon Spurgeon (1834–1892) comes to London as Pastor of the famous New Park Street Church, now known as the Metropolitan Tabernacle, Elephant and Castle.
1858	John Clifford (1836–1923) takes up the Pastorate at Paddington in West London, and Alexander MacLaren (1826–1910) settles in Manchester.
1879	W. Holman Bentley (1855–1905), explorer, missionary, and translator, sails for Congo (now Zaire).
1903	Baptist Church House is built as part of a forward movement initiated by Dr J. H. Shakespeare (1857–1928), General Secretary of the Baptist Union.
1905	The Baptist World Alliance is founded.
1922	R. Rowntree Clifford (1867–1943) sees the new buildings for the West Ham Central Mission brought into use.
1954	Dr Billy Graham (b. 1918) arrives in London for the first of his major evangelistic campaigns in Great Britain.
1968	Martin Luther King (b. 1929) is assassinated on 4 April.

Further Reading

Various books have already been mentioned in these pages, but the following list may also be helpful. Many of these books are now out of print but may be obtained from libraries or from a local Baptist minister.

SPECIALLY WRITTEN FOR YOUNG PEOPLE

Golden Foot by J. R. BATTEN. The story of Judson of Burma.

Crusader for Christ by JEAN WILSON. The story of Billy Graham. Both these books are in Lutterworth's *Faith and Fame* series.

POPULAR PAPERBACKS

Three Generations of Suffering by GEORGI VINS (Hodder and Stoughton).

Searchlight on Spurgeon by ERIC W. HAYDEN (obtainable from the author at Longhope Baptist Church, Gloucestershire, GL17 0PG.

Venture in Faith by P. ROWNTREE CLIFFORD (Carey Kingsgate Press 1950). The story of the West Ham Central Mission. Now out of print.

William Carey by J. B. MIDDLEBROOK (Baptist Missionary Society).

A History of the English Baptists by A. C. UNDER-
wood (Carey Kingsgate Press 1946).
A Bibliography of books on Baptist History by DAVID
KINGDON (obtainable from The Evangelical Library,
78a Chiltern Street, London W1).

Useful Addresses

The Baptist Union of Great Britain and Ireland, Baptist Times, and the London office of the Baptist World Alliance, are all housed at Baptist Church House, 4 Southampton Row, London WC1B 4AB.

The Baptist Union of Scotland, Baptist Church House, 14 Aytorn Road, Glasgow G41 5RT.

The Baptist Union of Wales, Ilston House, 94 Mansel Street, Swansea.

Baptist Union of Ireland, 3 Fitzwilliam Street, Belfast 9.

National Strict Baptist Federation, 5 Swiss Avenue, Watford, Herts.

The Baptist Missionary Society, 93–97 Gloucester Place, London WH1 4AA.

The Strict Baptist Mission, 61 Breakspears Road, London S.E.4.

Fellowship of Independent Evangelical Churches (F.I.E.C.), Fellowship House, 136 Rosendale Road, West Dulwich, London SE21 8LG.

'BAPTIST VIEW' SERIES
Authority by B. R. WHITE.
Baptism by J. F. MATTHEWS.
The Church by G. W. MARTIN.
The Ministry by J. F. V. NICHOLSON (all these are
    published by Baptist Publications).

FILMSTRIP
The Baptists (may be loaned from the Department of
    Mission, Baptist Church House).

USEFUL REFERENCE BOOKS
The Baptist Hymn Book Companion ed. HUGH
    MARTIN (Psalms and Hymns Trust, Baptist Church
    House).
Baptist Principles by H. WHEELER ROBINSON (Carey
    Kingsgate Press 1925).
The Life and Faith of the Baptists by H. WHEELER
    ROBINSON (Carey Kingsgate Press 1946).
What Baptists Stand For by HENRY COOK (Carey
    Kingsgate Press 1947).
Fellowship of Believers by E. A. PAYNE (Carey Kings-
    gate Press 1944).
The Free Church Tradition in the Life of England by
    E. A. PAYNE (Carey Kingsgate Press 1944).

FOR MUCH MORE ADVANCED STUDY
New Testament Doctrine of Baptism by W. F.
    FLEMINGTON (S.P.C.K. 1948).
Christian Baptism ed. A. GILMORE (Carey Kingsgate
    Press 1959).
Biblical Doctrine of Initiation by R. E. O. WHITE
    (Carey Kingsgate Press 1960).
The Pattern of the Church by A. GILMORE (Carey
    Kingsgate Press 1961).
The Gathered Community by ROBERT C. WALTON
    (Carey Kingsgate Press 1946).